Vision and Value

Evelyn Wright

Evelyn Wright

Index

Vision of the Perfect Product 7
Design for Excellence 13
Innovation and Differentiation 19
The Voice of the Customer 26
The Road to Quality 33
Quality Control and Operational Excellence 41
The DNA of a Company with Purpose 49
The Role of Inspirational Leadership 57
Companies that Transcend 65
Corporate Culture for the Common Good 73
Collaboration and Strategic Alliances 81
Key Elements of Sustainable Success 89
Innovation for Social Change 97
Measuring Social Impact 105
Beyond Sustainability 112
The Value of a Company in a Purpose-Driven Economy 119
Preparing the Next Generation of Conscious Entrepreneurs 126
Legacy 134

Vision of the Perfect Product

Creating a perfect product is much more than just having a good idea. It is a process that begins with a clear vision and a deep understanding of customer needs. The first step to achieving this is asking yourself the right questions: What problem are you trying to solve? Who needs this solution? Why will this product improve their lives? These questions seem simple, but answering them honestly and in detail is what will differentiate your product from a simple idea to a truly quality solution. It is not just about what you think the market needs, but what they are really looking for. The key is to put yourself in the customer's shoes and think from their perspective.

The vision of a perfect product doesn't come about overnight. It requires research, observation, and, above all, empathy. A common mistake is to assume that the creator always knows what's best. The reality is that the success of a product isn't determined by what you like, but by what resonates with the public. A perfect product is one that not only meets expectations, but exceeds them. It's anticipating the customer's needs before they even realize they have them. And to do that, it's essential to know the customer better than they know themselves.

Think about the great companies that have created iconic products. Apple, for example, didn't just launch a smartphone; it reinvented the way people interact with technology. Netflix didn't just create a platform for watching movies; it changed the way we consume entertainment. These products aren't perfect because they simply work well; they're perfect because they solve a problem in such a unique way that they become indispensable. And that's the key. To get to that vision of the perfect product, you have to go beyond what already exists. Innovation doesn't just mean making something new, but making it better, more efficient, and more satisfying for the customer.

A key aspect of achieving that vision is not settling for the obvious. Often, the most obvious solutions are not the best. Innovation often comes from questioning what seems unquestionable. If all the products in your category follow a pattern, ask yourself why. Is it because that is the only way to do it or because no one has dared to do something different? Dare to challenge the norms. Great innovations come from those who are not afraid to think differently.

Another important factor is simplicity. The perfect product is not necessarily the most complex one, but the one that offers a simple solution to a complicated problem. Often, product creators fall into the trap of adding unnecessary features, believing that more is better. But the reality is that too many features can confuse the user and take them away from what they really need. The perfect product focuses on the essentials, on what really makes the difference. It's not about how many features it has, but how well it solves the problem it was designed to solve.

Perfecting a product also involves a process of trial and error. No one achieves perfection on the first try. You need to launch prototypes, get feedback, and make constant improvements. This is where patience and persistence come into play. Every failure is an opportunity to learn, improve, and get closer to that vision of the perfect product. Don't be afraid to make mistakes, because every mistake will teach you a valuable lesson. The important thing is to have the humility to accept that there is always room for improvement.

One last key aspect is adaptability. The market changes, customer needs evolve, and what is relevant today might not be so tomorrow. That's why the vision of the perfect product needs to be flexible. You can't create something with the mindset that it will last forever in its current form. You need to be willing to adjust it, improve it, and adapt it to changes in the environment. History is full of products that were revolutionary in their time, but became obsolete because their creators were unable to adapt to new trends or technologies.

In short, the vision of the perfect product isn't just a brilliant idea. It's a constant commitment to innovation, simplicity, and customer satisfaction. It's understanding that it's not just about what you think is perfect, but what actually makes the customer's life easier, more efficient, or more enjoyable. It's a process that requires empathy, patience, and the ability to adapt. Only then can you get closer to creating something that's not just good, but truly perfect in the eyes of those who will use it.

Evelyn Wright

Design for Excellence

Designing for excellence is one of the most important pillars when it comes to creating a product that truly makes a difference. It is not enough to make something that simply works; the goal should be to create something that performs exceptionally, provides a unique user experience, and leaves a lasting impression on the customer. Design is not just about appearance or aesthetics, although these aspects are important. True design for excellence involves every detail, from how the product feels in the user's hands to how it performs under demanding conditions. Everything must be aligned to deliver the best quality possible.

The first step to designing a great product is to understand that design is not just about creativity, but about problem solving. Good design starts with a deep understanding of the problem you want to solve and the customer's expectations. This means that before you start creating any sketches or prototypes, you should spend time researching and analyzing. What are your customer's pain points? How can you make their lives easier? Design should be user-centered from the start, ensuring that every decision you make is motivated by the intention to improve the customer experience.

This is where the concept of functionality comes into play. A product can be beautiful, but if it doesn't work flawlessly, it will lose its value. Functionality should always be a priority. Every component, every piece, and every detail should have a clear purpose and enhance the overall functioning of the product. When you think about a functional design, you should ask yourself: How will the user interact with this product? How intuitive will it be? Does it efficiently respond to what the customer needs? A great product is one that the user can start using almost without reading a manual, because its design is so clear and logical that the experience flows naturally.

Another essential aspect of design excellence is the quality of materials. It doesn't matter how innovative or well thought out the concept is if the materials aren't up to par. Excellent design must be supported by high-quality materials that are durable, sustainable and convey a sense of value. Think about how a good product feels to the touch – smooth finishes, pleasant textures and the right weight give a sense of robustness and confidence. Don't underestimate the power of small details in design. The type of material, the choice of colours and even the way a button sounds when pressed can influence a customer's perception of quality.

In addition to functionality and materials, designing for excellence also involves a focus on simplicity. Sometimes, less is more. A common mistake is to overload the product with unnecessary features or elements that only end up complicating its use. Simplicity is the path to excellence. This means that you must be able to distill the essence of the product, removing everything that does not provide real value. Good design is clear, direct, and avoids distractions. When you manage to create something that is simple to use, but at the same time offers a powerful solution, you are reaching a level of excellence that few products achieve.

Attention to detail is another key aspect of designing for excellence. It's easy to focus on the big, obvious elements, but the small details are what really make the difference between a good product and an exceptional one. Every angle, every curve, and every interaction must be precisely thought out. From the way the product is packaged to how the user feels when opening it, it's all part of the experience. The best products are those that surprise the customer at every step, that offer something more than what was expected, and they achieve this through careful, detailed design.

You can't talk about design for excellence without mentioning sustainability. In today's world, where environmental impact is a growing concern, design must also consider its ecological footprint. Products that are designed with the environment in mind are not only better for the planet, but they also resonate more with conscious consumers. Using recyclable materials, reducing waste, and creating products that are easy to repair and not throw away are practices that should be integrated into the design process. Excellent design not only meets immediate customer needs, but also has a positive impact in the long term.

Finally, designing for excellence is not a process that ends once the product hits the market. It is a continuous cycle of improvement. There will always be room to make adjustments, improve features, and optimize the user experience. Customer feedback is invaluable in this regard. You must be open to hearing what works and what doesn't, and be willing to make changes if necessary. Excellence is not something that is achieved immediately, but is built over time, with effort, and with a constant commitment to improvement.

In short, designing for excellence means going beyond expectations. It's putting the user at the center of every decision, focusing on functionality, simplicity, quality materials, sustainability, and the details that really matter. It's a process that requires dedication, patience, and a clear vision of what it means to create something that's not just good, but truly excellent. When you manage to combine all of these elements, the result is a product that not only meets, but exceeds, and leaves a lasting impression on those who use it.

Innovation and Differentiation

Innovation and differentiation are two fundamental concepts that every product developer must understand if they want to stand out in a competitive market. Innovation doesn't simply mean inventing something new, but finding creative ways to improve what already exists or solve a problem in a different and more effective way. And differentiation, on the other hand, is what will make your product stand out from the competition. In a world full of similar products, the key to success is to offer something that is unique, memorable and adds real value to the customer.

Innovation starts with the ability to observe and question what others take for granted. Often, the best ideas come not from inventing from scratch, but from improving what is already on the market. Think of great innovations in history: The automobile was not the first means of transportation, but it was a revolutionary improvement over horses and buggies. The iPhone was not the first phone, but it radically changed the way we interact with technology. Innovation is that shift in perspective, that ability to see beyond what is and envision what could be.

The first step to innovation is to identify a problem or need that isn't being addressed in the best way possible. Problems are everywhere; you just need to look closely. What makes customers' lives more difficult? What frustrations do they experience with current products? These questions are essential to finding starting points for innovation. It's not just about improving existing features, but about thinking of completely new ways to solve problems.

Once you've identified an opportunity to innovate, the next challenge is to differentiate your product. This is where many fall short. It's not enough to just offer something new; you have to make sure that what you're offering is different and valuable enough for the customer to notice. Differentiation is based on the principle that if your product is the same as all the others, consumers will have no reason to choose you. So what can you do to make your product not just another one on the shelf?

Differentiation can be achieved in many ways. One of the most effective ways is through design. A product that looks different, feels different, and is used differently will automatically attract attention. However, it's not just about aesthetics; it's also about functionality. Your product should be easy to use, intuitive, and above all, it should solve a problem more efficiently than anything else on the market. That's the real difference. The customer doesn't just want something that looks good, they want something that makes their life better.

Another way to differentiate is through customer experience. This goes beyond the product itself. What is the experience like from the moment the customer sees your product to when they use it? This is where the most successful brands really stand out. Apple, for example, doesn't just sell phones; it sells an entire experience. From the design of its stores to the ease of setting up a new device, everything is designed to make the customer feel special. That's a powerful form of differentiation – creating an experience so unique that customers won't want to go anywhere else.

Innovation and differentiation also require courage. Often, innovation means moving away from what is safe or proven. It means taking risks. When you decide to do something different, there is always the possibility that it won't work out the way you expected. But the fear of failure shouldn't stop you. In fact, mistakes are part of the innovation process. Every failure is an opportunity to learn and improve. The most innovative companies aren't afraid of making mistakes; they see each mistake as another step toward success. This trial-and-error approach is what ultimately leads to great innovations.

It's also important to mention that differentiation isn't always about the product itself. Sometimes, it's the business model that makes you different. Netflix, for example, didn't invent movies or TV shows, but it changed the way we consume them by offering a subscription model instead of renting or buying. Uber didn't invent transportation, but it revolutionized the industry by creating a platform that connects drivers with passengers instantly. These examples show that you don't always have to invent a new product to innovate. Sometimes, all you need to do is change the way it's offered or distributed.

The key to innovation and differentiation is to always stay one step ahead. The market doesn't wait, and what's innovative today may become obsolete tomorrow. That's why it's essential to be constantly evolving. Innovation isn't something that happens once and that's it. It's a continuous process. You have to be willing to constantly question what you're doing, challenge the norms, and look for new ways to improve. You can't settle for current success; you have to always be looking for what's next.

Another essential part of innovation is keeping an eye on technological and social trends. The world is constantly changing, and products that don't adapt to these changes quickly fall behind. The most innovative companies are those that see trends coming before others do. Whether it's the rise of artificial intelligence, sustainability, or changes in consumer behavior, you should always be aware of what's happening in the world. This will allow you to not only stay up to date, but also seize new opportunities before your competition.

In short, innovation and differentiation are key to creating a product that truly stands out in the market. It's not just about doing something new, but doing it better and differently. The key is to observe, identify problems, think creatively and not be afraid to take risks. Differentiation, on the other hand, ensures that your product is unique and memorable, whether through its design, its functionality or the experience it offers to the customer. Innovating and differentiating is an ongoing process that requires effort, creativity and, above all, a clear vision of what you want to achieve. When you manage to combine these elements, the result is a product that is not only successful in the market, but also leaves a lasting mark on the minds of consumers.

The Voice of the Customer

Listening to the voice of the customer is one of the most important pillars to creating a quality product and a successful company. Often, companies focus on what they think is best, instead of paying attention to what their customers really need. And that's a mistake. The customer is the one who uses the product, who lives the experience, and therefore, has the best perspective on what works and what doesn't. Ignoring their opinion is like walking blindly, hoping everything will turn out well. If you want to create something that is truly useful, valuable, and resonates with the public, you have to listen to what they have to say.

But listening to the voice of the customer isn't just about collecting data or conducting surveys. It's about deeply understanding their needs, desires, and frustrations. Customers, in their day-to-day lives, encounter small problems or inconveniences that designers or product creators often don't anticipate. That's why their feedback is so valuable: it allows you to adjust, improve, and refine your product so that it actually solves those problems. Listening to your customers gives you a competitive advantage, because it allows you to offer something that is more aligned with what they're really looking for.

One of the most common mistakes companies make is assuming they know their customers better than they know themselves. They may think they know what's best for them, but the reality is that only the customer knows what really works for them. It's not enough to rely on assumptions or what internal teams think is best. The companies that thrive are those that take the time to listen, observe, and learn from their customers on a constant basis. This doesn't mean you should change your vision or give in to every demand, but it does mean you should be flexible and willing to make adjustments when necessary.

The process of listening to your customers needs to be active and ongoing. It's not enough to just conduct an occasional survey or check online reviews from time to time. You need to establish open and accessible communication channels for customers to voice their opinions on an ongoing basis. This can be through regular surveys, focus groups, social media comment analysis, or even dedicated feedback platforms. The important thing is to make sure that customers know that their opinions are valued and that you are willing to act on them.

One of the great benefits of listening to the voice of the customer is that it not only helps you improve your product, but also build a stronger relationship with them. Customers feel valued when they see that a company listens to them and takes their opinions into account. This builds loyalty and trust. When customers feel that they are part of the process of creating or improving the product, they are more likely to remain loyal to the brand and recommend the product to others. Deep down, people want to feel that they are heard and that their opinions matter. Giving them that opportunity strengthens the relationship between the company and the customer.

Sometimes, listening to the voice of the customer can lead to surprising discoveries. Maybe customers use your product in ways you never imagined, or maybe they have ideas for improvement that you would never have thought of. These are golden opportunities to innovate and differentiate yourself in the marketplace. Don't underestimate the value of the creativity that customers can bring to the table. Often, it's those on the "battlefield," using the product daily, who have the brightest ideas about how to improve it.

It's also important to remember that not all feedback will be positive, and that's okay. Criticism, while it can sometimes be hard to hear, is an invaluable source of learning. Instead of ignoring it or taking it personally, you should view it as an opportunity to improve. If a customer has a bad experience, ask yourself what went wrong and how you can fix it. Criticism allows you to see the weak points of your product or service and gives you the opportunity to fix them before they affect more people. In fact, some of the best product innovations and improvements have come from customer feedback.

However, listening to the voice of the customer doesn't mean you should make radical changes every time someone suggests it. You need to be able to balance customer feedback with your vision and the direction you want to take as a company. Sometimes, customers may ask for things that, while seeming good in the short term, aren't sustainable or aligned with your brand's long-term values. This is where your judgment as a leader comes into play. Listening is key, but you need to be able to filter and discern which feedback actually adds value and which may be counterproductive.

Another important aspect is personalization. By listening to your customers, you can begin to identify patterns and trends in their needs and preferences. This allows you to customize the product or service more effectively. Personalization is one of the keys to making customers feel like the product is made specifically for them. Not all customers are the same, and while you can't personalize every detail for each person, you can adjust certain aspects for groups of customers with similar needs. This personalization can be the difference between a satisfied customer and a delighted one.

Finally, listening to customers also helps you adapt to changes in the market. Consumer needs and expectations change over time, and what worked a few years ago may not be enough today. If you're not paying attention to what customers are saying, you can quickly fall behind. Changes in technologies, cultural trends, or consumer priorities can have a huge impact on what they look for in a product or service. Staying on top of their opinions allows you to be agile and adapt to those changes quickly and effectively.

In conclusion, listening to the voice of the customer is one of the best tools you have at your disposal to create a successful product and a company that truly connects with its audience. It's not just about asking for feedback, but about learning from it, adapting, and continually improving. The customer is the heart of any business, and their feedback is what will guide you to make something that is not just good, but exceptional. When you manage to integrate that feedback into your development process, you create something that not only satisfies a need, but creates a lasting and meaningful connection with those who use it.

The Road to Quality

The road to quality is a journey that every business must undertake if it wants to be successful and earn the trust of its customers. Quality is not something that is achieved overnight, nor is it a goal that is achieved once and then forgotten. It is an ongoing commitment that requires effort, dedication, and attention to detail at every step of the process. Quality not only defines the product or service you offer, but also the reputation of your brand and the relationship you build with your customers. Simply put, quality is the foundation on which successful businesses are built.

The first step on the road to quality is to understand that quality is non-negotiable. In a competitive market, customers have many options, and if your product doesn't meet their quality expectations, they're likely to move on to another brand that does. That's why, from the moment you start developing a product, quality should be at the heart of every decision you make. It's not just about meeting minimum standards, but going above and beyond to ensure that every aspect of your product is the best it can be.

Quality starts with planning. Before you even get down to business, you need to have a clear vision of what you want to achieve. What defines a quality product in your industry? What are your customers' expectations? These are key questions that should guide your design and production process. Good planning involves thinking through every detail, from the materials you'll use to the manufacturing processes. If you take the time to plan well from the start, you'll be that much closer to achieving a product that truly meets the quality standards you've set for yourself.

Another important aspect in the quest for quality is the choice of materials. The materials you use have a direct impact on the durability, function, and appearance of your product. You cannot expect to offer a high-quality product if you are using low-quality materials. This is where many companies try to cut costs, but it is a mistake that can end up costing you dearly in the long run. Investing in good materials is one of the best decisions you can make if you want to create a product that really stands out in the market. A well-made product, with solid materials, will not only have a better lifespan, but will also convey confidence to the customer.

Manufacturing is also a key factor on the road to quality. It doesn't matter how good your materials are if the manufacturing process isn't up to par. Every step of the production process must be controlled to ensure that the final product is consistent and of high quality. This is where precision and attention to detail play a critical role. Machines must be well calibrated, workers must be trained, and quality controls must be rigorous. Every piece that comes off the production line must be carefully checked to ensure that it meets the set standards.

Quality control is, in fact, a vital part of this journey. It is not just about checking the product at the end of the process, but rather implementing it at every stage of development and production. Quality controls should be an ongoing practice, from the selection of materials to the final assembly. By doing this, you not only reduce the possibility of errors, but you also ensure that any problems are detected and fixed before they reach the customer. This not only protects the integrity of your product, but also the reputation of your company.

Quality isn't limited to the physical product, though. It also encompasses customer service, the shopping experience, packaging, and delivery. A customer can receive the best product in the world, but if their experience with your company is subpar, they're unlikely to buy from you again. Quality should permeate every aspect of your business. Customer service should be fast, efficient, and always focused on solving problems. Packaging should adequately protect the product and give an impression of professionalism and care. And delivery should be fast and hassle-free. All of these details add to the overall quality perception that customers have of your brand.

The journey to quality also requires a focus on continuous improvement. You can't just sit back once you achieve a certain level of quality. There's always something that can be improved. This may mean updating your manufacturing processes, improving materials, or even revising product design to make it more efficient. The market changes, customer expectations evolve, and technology advances. If you're not willing to constantly adapt and improve, you're likely to fall behind. Quality isn't a destination, it's a journey that never ends.

Furthermore, quality isn't just about what you can measure or see. It's also about the subjective experience of the customer. How do they feel when they use your product? Do they find it easy to use? Is it pleasing to the eye and touch? These are questions that go beyond numbers and technical controls, but they are equally important. Quality, ultimately, is a combination of tangible and intangible factors. It's an overall perception that the customer has that can make or break your product's reputation.

One aspect that cannot be overlooked on the road to quality is the culture within your company. If your employees are not committed to quality, it is difficult to achieve products that truly reflect it. You must create a culture where everyone, from the manager to the worker on the production line, is focused on doing things right. This involves training, constant communication, and a work environment where excellence is valued. When each member of the team understands the importance of quality and is willing to do their part, the results are tangible.

Ultimately, quality is what builds trust. Customers return to buy products they trust – products they know work well, are durable, and deliver on their promises. Quality is what transforms a casual customer into a loyal customer. And that loyalty is what drives long-term growth for any business. Don't underestimate the power of a well-made product. Recommendations, positive reviews, and a good reputation are built on quality, and all of that, in turn, translates into sales, success, and sustained growth.

In short, the path to quality is a continuous process that spans from initial planning to the customer experience after purchase. It's not just about doing things right once, but doing them right every time, at every stage and in every detail. Quality is what separates great companies from mediocre ones, and it's what makes customers trust you and come back again and again. If you commit to following this path, you will not only have a successful product, but also a brand that earns the respect and loyalty of its customers.

Quality Control and Operational Excellence

Quality control and operational excellence are two concepts that go hand in hand when it comes to ensuring that a product or service meets the highest standards. These elements don't just focus on the end result, but encompass every step of the process, from the acquisition of raw materials to the delivery of the finished product to the customer. Achieving operational excellence means optimizing every phase of production and management, while quality control ensures that what you offer meets expectations, both internal and external. Together, they are the key to delivering a flawless, reliable product that earns the trust of your customers.

Quality control is essential because it establishes a system of constant surveillance during the production process. It is not enough to have good materials or an innovative design if you do not guarantee that, at the end of the process, everything is in order. This control involves checking every detail, detecting errors before they reach the customer, and ensuring that all products meet established specifications. In practice, this means carrying out periodic tests and detailed analysis at different points in the production chain. If any part fails the controls, it must be corrected immediately to prevent failures from multiplying.

Implementing a good quality control system not only reduces defects, but also saves you time and money in the long run. While it may seem like adding testing and controls at every stage of the process increases costs, the reality is that it prevents bigger problems down the road. Think of the amount of resources that would be wasted if a defective product were to reach the market. Not only would you lose money on returns and repairs, but also your reputation. Customer trust is fragile, and a preventable mistake can have a lasting impact on your brand. That's why quality control is not an expense, but a smart investment.

Furthermore, quality control is not just the responsibility of the production department. Every employee should feel responsible for ensuring that quality standards are met at all times. From workers on the assembly line to managers, everyone has a role in this process. This is where company culture plays a crucial role.

If quality is part of your company's DNA, then each person will understand the importance of their job within the grand scheme. When everyone in the organization is aligned with the goal of delivering high-quality products, the end result is much more likely to be excellent.

Operational excellence is the next step in this process. It's about taking efficiency and quality to the next level. Unlike quality control, which focuses on reviewing and ensuring that the product meets standards, operational excellence seeks to optimize every part of the system. This means eliminating waste, improving production times, reducing errors, and making everything work more quickly and efficiently. Operational excellence involves looking at every process and asking, "How can we do this better?" It's not just about meeting expectations, but exceeding them.

Achieving operational excellence requires a strategic approach and a continuous improvement mindset. It is not about making drastic changes overnight, but about fine-tuning and perfecting each area, step by step. Here it is important to use analysis and management tools such as Lean Manufacturing or Six Sigma, which help identify inefficiencies and find data-driven solutions. These methodologies provide a systematic approach to improving processes, eliminating what does not add value and maximizing performance. The goal is to make the entire system more efficient, without compromising quality.

In the pursuit of operational excellence, technology plays a key role. Companies that excel in this area often integrate automated systems and management software that allows them to have greater control over every aspect of production. Technology not only speeds up processes, but also reduces the margin of error, as machines tend to be more accurate and consistent than humans in certain tasks. However, it is important that technology does not replace human supervision. Automated systems must work hand-in-hand with people to ensure that everything is working as it should.

One of the fundamental principles of operational excellence is continuous improvement. It is not enough to achieve a high level of efficiency and quality; you must always look for ways to improve. Even when a system seems to be working well, there are always areas that can be optimized. This preventive approach prevents problems from accumulating and allows your company to stay competitive in an ever-changing market. Customers value not only quality, but also innovation. And a company that is constantly improving its processes is better positioned to adapt and offer ever-improving products.

One aspect that is often overlooked when talking about quality control and operational excellence is the impact they have on customer satisfaction. By ensuring that products are consistent, reliable, and well-made, you are building a relationship of trust with your customers. They know they can count on your brand to deliver what you promise. Plus, when a company is excellent at its operation, delivery times are faster, prices are often more competitive, and the overall customer experience is improved. All of this translates into loyalty and referrals, which are crucial for long-term growth.

Another important benefit of operational excellence is cost reduction. By optimizing processes and eliminating inefficiencies, you can produce more with fewer resources. Not only does this improve profitability, but it also allows you to offer higher quality products at more competitive prices. And in a market where consumers are looking for the best value for their money, this is a huge differentiator. Operational excellence gives you a competitive advantage that is hard to match by companies that do not invest in continually improving their operations.

Finally, it is important to understand that both quality control and operational excellence are processes that require long-term commitment. It is not about implementing a system and then forgetting about it. You must be constantly reviewing, adjusting and improving. The market changes, technologies advance and customer expectations evolve. If you are not willing to adapt and seek continuous improvement, you will be left behind. The most successful companies are those that never stop looking for ways to be better, more efficient and more relevant to their customers.

In conclusion, quality control and operational excellence are two sides of the same coin. While quality control makes sure your product meets standards and expectations, operational excellence ensures that the entire system is running optimally. Together, they form the basis of a business that is not only efficient and profitable, but also reliable and able to deliver products that truly make a difference in customers' lives. If you want to build a successful company in the long term, these two principles must be at the heart of your strategy.

The DNA of a Company with Purpose

The DNA of a purpose-driven company is what defines it beyond its product or service. It is that inner essence that guides every decision, every action, and every interaction, both with customers and employees and society at large. While many companies focus exclusively on profits, a purpose-driven company has a deeper mission. It seeks not only to make a profit, but also to make a positive impact on the world. This purpose becomes the engine that drives the company, gives it a sense of direction, and connects it emotionally with the people who interact with it.

To build a purpose-driven business, the first thing you need to do is clearly define what your mission is. This can't just be an empty statement, written to adorn the office walls or appear on the website. It has to be an authentic mission, something that truly represents the values and principles you believe in as an entrepreneur. Purpose needs to go beyond the idea of selling products or services. It needs to answer a fundamental question: how does your business contribute to improving the lives of people or the planet? The answer to this question is at the heart of your purpose-driven business's DNA.

A clear example of a purpose-driven company is one that seeks to solve a social or environmental problem through its products. Imagine a company that makes eco-friendly cleaning products. Its purpose is not just to clean homes and offices, but to do so in a way that minimizes environmental impact. This company has a purpose that is aligned with a greater cause: protecting the environment. Through its products, it educates consumers about the damage that traditional products can cause to the ecosystem, and offers them an alternative that not only fulfills its function, but also contributes to the preservation of the planet. In this case, purpose becomes the company's reason for being, and that is what distinguishes it from other companies in the same sector.

Purpose must be present in every corner of the organization, from the biggest decisions to the smallest details of everyday life. It is not enough to have a good intention or a nice phrase in your mission. Purpose has to be reflected in concrete actions. A company with a purpose takes care of its employees, offers fair working conditions and promotes well-being within its team. Employees are the first ambassadors of the mission, and if they do not feel that the company is committed to that purpose, it is likely that that mission will not be reflected externally. Therefore, it is essential that all levels of the company are aligned with that mission and that they feel part of something bigger.

Another key aspect of a purpose-driven company's DNA is transparency. Companies that truly have a purpose have nothing to hide. They are honest and clear about their practices, their goals, and the challenges they face. This transparency builds trust both inside and outside the organization. Customers value honesty, and if a company is open about its efforts to fulfill its purpose, even when facing difficulties, consumers are much more likely to feel emotionally connected to the brand. What's more, this transparency also helps build stronger relationships with partners and suppliers who share the same values.

A purpose-driven company also knows that its success is not measured only in terms of financial profits. Of course, profits are important for the sustainability of any business, but a purpose-driven company measures its success more broadly. The social or environmental impact it generates is equally relevant. This mindset changes the way goals are set and decisions are made. Instead of just seeking to maximize short-term profits, the company seeks to balance its financial achievements with its positive contribution to the world. Success is measured by the impact it has on the lives of customers, the communities where the company operates, and the planet.

Purpose also has the power to create a deep connection between a company and its customers. In a world where consumers have more and more choices, purpose becomes a differentiating factor. People don't just want to buy a product; they want to support companies that align with their values. When a company has a clear and genuine purpose, it attracts customers who share those ideals. Not only does this strengthen customer loyalty, it also transforms the relationship between the company and the consumer into more than just a transaction. It becomes a community of people working together toward a common goal.

But purpose should not be static. As the world changes and new challenges arise, businesses must also adapt. Purpose should be flexible, allowing the business to evolve without losing its essence. This does not mean that the mission must change radically, but it does mean that the business must be willing to adjust its approaches and strategies to remain relevant in an ever-changing environment. A purpose-driven business is resilient because it is driven by a mission larger than itself. This mission gives it the strength to overcome obstacles and adapt to new realities.

Furthermore, purpose is not just something that benefits the company. It also has a significant impact on the people who work there. When employees feel like they are part of something meaningful, their motivation and job satisfaction increase. Working for a company whose sole objective is to generate profit is not the same as working for a company that has a higher purpose. When employees see that their work contributes to a greater cause, they feel a greater sense of pride and belonging. This, in turn, translates into a more engaged and productive team. Purpose not only improves relationships with customers, but also with employees, creating a more positive and satisfying work environment.

Ultimately, the DNA of a purpose-driven company is much more than a slogan or a marketing strategy. It is a way of doing business that puts people, the planet and social well-being at the heart of its decisions. It is a constant commitment to something bigger than profits, a way of positively contributing to the world while building a successful company. A purpose-driven company is aware of its impact and is determined to use its influence to create real change. It is a company that inspires, that creates genuine connections and that ultimately leaves a lasting mark on society.

Building a purpose-driven company takes time, effort, and dedication, but the benefits are incalculable. Not only will you be creating a stronger, more resilient company, but one that truly makes a difference in the world. And that's the kind of legacy worth leaving behind. A purpose-driven company doesn't just survive; it thrives, because it's connected to something much deeper than the numbers on a balance sheet. It's connected to humanity and the need to build a better future for all.

The Role of Inspirational Leadership

The role of inspirational leadership is crucial to the success of any company, especially if it is defined by a purpose that goes beyond profits. An inspirational leader is not simply someone who gives orders or makes important decisions. He or she is someone who guides, motivates and, above all, inspires the people around him or her. This type of leadership is not about imposing power, but about creating an environment where people want to give their best, not because they are forced to, but because they feel part of something bigger.

An inspiring leader has the ability to communicate a clear and compelling vision. This vision should not only be realistic and achievable, but also exciting. It should resonate with the team and align with the company's values. When a leader is able to effectively articulate where the company is headed and why it is important, employees not only understand what is expected of them, but are also motivated to work with passion. The vision gives them a sense of direction, something to strive for, and helps them see how their efforts contribute to the organization's success.

However, inspiration is not just about talking nice or giving exciting speeches. An inspiring leader leads by example. This means that their actions must be aligned with their words. There is nothing more demotivating for a team than seeing their leader act contrary to what they preach. If a leader talks about commitment, but does not show commitment; or if they talk about ethics, but make questionable decisions, they will quickly lose the trust and respect of their team. On the other hand, when a leader acts in a way that is consistent with the company's values and the vision they have communicated, they earn the respect and loyalty of their employees. Consistency between word and action is key to inspiring leadership.

Empathy is another key characteristic of an inspiring leader. A good leader knows that his or her team is made up of people with different needs, emotions, and situations. Being empathetic means being able to put yourself in other people's shoes, understand their challenges, and offer support when needed. A leader who shows empathy creates a more humane work environment, where employees feel valued not only for what they do, but also for who they are. This type of emotional connection not only improves team morale, but also strengthens commitment and loyalty to the company.

Another important aspect of inspirational leadership is the ability to foster trust. Without trust, there can be no true leadership. Employees must feel that they can trust their leader, not only to make wise decisions, but also to be honest and transparent. A leader who is open and candid, even in difficult times, builds a strong foundation of trust. Trust is the glue that holds a team together, especially in times of uncertainty or change. And when employees trust their leader, they are much more likely to stay engaged and willing to give their best.

In addition, an inspiring leader encourages collaboration and teamwork. It is not about being a central figure who makes all the decisions and carries all the weight on his shoulders. On the contrary, a good leader knows that success does not depend on a single person, but on collective effort. He fosters an environment where ideas flow freely, where diversity of thought is valued and where each team member has the opportunity to contribute. An inspiring leader is not afraid to surround himself with talented people and allow them to shine. In fact, by empowering his team and giving them the freedom to make decisions, the leader strengthens the cohesion and creativity of the group.

A leader's ability to manage change is also a vital component of inspirational leadership. We live in a world that is constantly evolving, and companies must adapt quickly to stay competitive. A leader who can guide their team through change, keeping them focused and motivated, is invaluable. However, managing change does not mean imposing it abruptly. An inspirational leader understands that change can create anxiety and resistance, so they make sure to clearly communicate why it is necessary and how it will benefit the company and the team in the long run. They also offer support during the transition and are available to address questions or concerns. In this way, the team feels more confident and prepared to face new challenges.

An inspiring leader must also be an excellent communicator. Clear, open, and honest communication is essential to building a positive and productive work environment. A leader who communicates effectively ensures that everyone on the team understands not only their responsibilities, but also how their work connects to the company's overall goals. Additionally, open communication encourages two-way feedback. A good leader doesn't just talk, but also listens. They value their team's opinions and suggestions, and are willing to make adjustments when necessary. This ability to listen not only improves relationships within the team, but also leads to better decisions and more creative solutions.

Resilience is another important quality in an inspiring leader. Leaders constantly face challenges, both internal and external, and the ability to bounce back from setbacks is essential. A leader who displays resilience doesn't let failures or difficulties get him or her down. Instead, he or she sees them as opportunities to learn and improve. This positive, proactive attitude inspires his or her team to do the same. When employees see their leader staying strong and optimistic in the midst of adversity, they are more likely to adopt a resilient mindset as well. Resilience is contagious, and an inspiring leader spreads it to his or her entire team.

Additionally, an inspiring leader recognizes and celebrates achievements, both big and small. Recognition is a powerful tool to keep the team motivated. It's not just about financial rewards or bonuses. Sometimes a simple, sincere thank you or public acknowledgement can have a much deeper impact. Employees who feel valued and appreciated for their work are more engaged and productive. A leader who takes the time to recognize the efforts of their team creates a positive environment where people feel motivated to continue giving their best.

Finally, an inspiring leader has a genuine commitment to the growth and development of his team. He doesn't see his employees as mere resources, but as people with potential. He makes sure to provide development opportunities, whether through training, mentoring, or new challenges. A good leader invests in the growth of his team because he knows that when employees grow, so does the company. By fostering an environment where learning and development are a priority, the leader not only inspires his team to continually improve, but also strengthens the company's ability to innovate and adapt to change.

In short, inspirational leadership is much more than making decisions and leading a team. It is the ability to motivate, guide and empower people to give their best. An inspirational leader is one who communicates a clear vision, acts with integrity, shows empathy, fosters collaboration and trust, and manages change effectively. This is someone who not only seeks the success of the company, but also the well-being and growth of their team. In an increasingly competitive business world, inspirational leadership becomes a key advantage to create organizations that not only survive, but thrive and generate a positive impact on their employees and society.

Companies that Transcend

Companies that transcend are those that go beyond simply fulfilling their basic function of selling products or services. They are the ones that leave a deep mark on society, those that remain relevant over time and those that manage to be remembered by generations. These companies do not only focus on financial results, but also have a broader purpose that drives them to improve the world in some way. In a market where many companies come and go, those that manage to transcend do so because they have known how to connect with something deeper: with people, with society, and with the values that really matter.

For a company to succeed, the first thing it must do is clearly define its purpose. This purpose must go beyond simply making money. Sure, profits are important, but a company that succeeds doesn't focus solely on that. These companies ask themselves: what value are we bringing to the world? How are we making our customers' lives better? The answers to these questions form the core of their purpose. Once that purpose is defined, it becomes the compass that guides all of their decisions. Whether it's creating new products, the way they treat their employees, or how they interact with their customers, everything is aligned with that purpose.

Companies that thrive are also those that understand that their success depends on the relationships they build. It's not just about selling products and services, but about creating genuine connections with people. These companies focus on building long-term relationships with their customers, employees, and communities. They know that a relationship based on trust and respect is much more valuable than a quick transaction. This human connection is what allows them to thrive and stay relevant in a world that is constantly changing. Companies that thrive listen to their customers, value their opinions, and adapt to their needs.

Innovation also plays a crucial role in a company's transcendence. Transcendent companies don't get stuck on a single formula for success. They understand that the world is constantly changing, and they are willing to evolve with it. Innovation doesn't always mean creating something completely new, it can be improving what already exists, adapting it to new realities, or finding more efficient ways of doing things. Transcendent companies are constantly looking for ways to improve, whether it's their products, their processes, or the way they operate. This continuous improvement mindset allows them to stay ahead and remain relevant, even when the market changes.

Another key characteristic of companies that transcend is that they have a strong sense of social responsibility. These companies not only care about their own profits, but they also care about the impact they have on society and the environment. They understand that they are part of a larger ecosystem and that their actions have consequences. Companies that transcend are those that are committed to doing the right thing, even when it is not the easiest or most profitable thing to do in the short term. This commitment to the common good not only helps them gain the loyalty of their customers, but it also gives them a reason for being that transcends time.

Furthermore, companies that thrive understand the importance of adapting to change without losing their core. The business world is constantly evolving, and companies that fail to adapt risk being left behind. But adapting doesn't mean abandoning what makes them unique. Companies that thrive find ways to stay true to their core values while navigating market changes, new technologies, and shifting consumer demands. This flexibility is what allows them to survive and thrive over time.

Leadership is also an essential factor in companies that succeed. The leaders of these companies are visionaries, people who see beyond immediate success and are committed to long-term growth. They are leaders who inspire their employees and motivate them to work towards a common goal. But beyond being visionaries, these leaders are also humble. They know that they cannot achieve success on their own, and they value the contribution of each team member. Good leadership creates a work culture where each person feels valued and motivated, which in turn strengthens the company and allows it to succeed.

Organizational culture is another determining factor in companies that succeed. These companies have cultures that promote collaboration, innovation, and respect. Employees at these companies don't just see their work as a job, but as an opportunity to contribute to something bigger. Instead of simply fulfilling their responsibilities, they feel part of a larger mission. This positive culture not only increases productivity, but also helps attract and retain top talent. A strong organizational culture is one of the pillars that sustain a company that succeeds.

On the other hand, companies that transcend understand the importance of sustainability. In a world where natural resources are limited and climate change is a reality, companies that truly care about the future look for ways to operate more sustainably. This means reducing their carbon footprint, using recyclable materials, and making sure their operations do not harm the environment. These companies are not just looking for short-term success, but are committed to creating a better future for generations to come. This commitment to sustainability not only gives them a competitive advantage, but also allows them to positively contribute to the world.

Finally, companies that transcend are not afraid to leave a legacy. They are not concerned only with immediate results, but rather think about the impact they will have in the long term. These companies are building something that will endure, something that will continue to exist long after their founders are gone. This legacy is not measured only in financial terms, but in how the company has improved people's lives, contributed to the well-being of society, and made a difference in the world. Companies that transcend leave an indelible mark, not only on the economy, but on the culture, on the lives of their employees, and on the way business is done.

In short, the companies that transcend are those that understand that true success is not measured by numbers alone. They are the ones that have found a deeper purpose, built genuine relationships, adapted and innovated, and made a positive impact on the world. These companies not only survive, but thrive over time, leaving a legacy that endures and continues to inspire others. In a world where companies come and go, the ones that transcend are the ones that truly make a difference.

Evelyn Wright

Corporate Culture for the Common Good

Corporate culture is the lifeblood of a company. It defines how employees behave, how decisions are made, and how the company interacts with the outside world. A corporate culture that is geared toward the common good goes beyond generating profits or achieving financial goals. It is about creating an environment in which every decision, every action, and every interaction is guided by principles that benefit not only the company, but society as a whole. This focus on the common good transforms companies into agents of positive change, with an impact that transcends the walls of the office.

In a corporate culture for the common good, social purpose is at the heart of everything we do. This means that the company does not just focus on being profitable, but actively seeks out how it can meaningfully contribute to the well-being of the community, employees, and the planet. Every member of the organization, from the most senior executive to the newest employee, understands that their actions must align with this greater purpose. It is not just about doing what is legal or complying with regulations, but about going above and beyond and acting in an ethical, responsible, and supportive manner at all times.

The first step in building a corporate culture focused on the common good is to create an inclusive and respectful work environment. In these types of companies, each person feels valued for who they are, not just for what they can do. Diversity is not just a concept mentioned in corporate documents, but a reality that is lived every day. Companies that promote a culture for the common good understand that diversity of ideas, experiences, and perspectives is an invaluable source of creativity and innovation. In addition, these companies know that when people feel valued, they work with more passion and dedication.

But inclusion isn't just about hiring people from different backgrounds. It also involves creating an environment where every person feels heard and has the opportunity to grow. This means that rigid hierarchies have no place in a culture geared toward the common good. Instead of imposing decisions from the top down, these companies encourage participation and dialogue. Everyone has a voice, and the input of each team member is valued. This not only improves decision-making, but also strengthens employees' sense of belonging and engagement.

Empathy is another fundamental pillar of a corporate culture for the common good. In a business world that often moves quickly and where numbers seem to be the only thing that matters, the companies that transcend are those that know how to stop and consider the human impact of each decision. These companies understand that behind every number there are people: employees, customers, suppliers and communities. Acting with empathy means caring about the well-being of others and making an effort to understand their needs and challenges. This ability to put oneself in the shoes of others is what allows companies to build stronger and longer-lasting relationships with all their stakeholders.

In addition to fostering an inclusive and empathetic environment, companies with a culture for the common good also care about the personal and professional development of their employees. They do not see people just as resources that help achieve goals, but as individuals with unique potential. These companies invest in the training and growth of their team, offering training, mentoring and skills development opportunities. In doing so, they not only improve their employees' ability to contribute to the company, but also help them achieve their own personal goals and aspirations. This creates a virtuous circle in which motivated and satisfied employees give their best, which in turn benefits the company and society.

Another essential aspect of a corporate culture for the common good is the commitment to sustainability and the environment. Companies that operate under this principle understand that they cannot prosper in the long term if they do not take care of the planet. This translates into concrete actions such as reducing resource use, minimizing waste, investing in clean energy, and developing products or services that are environmentally friendly. In addition, these companies strive to educate their employees and customers about the importance of sustainability, encouraging a change in mindset that can have a much greater impact.

Ethics is a core value in a culture geared toward the common good. In a business environment where pressure for quick results can lead to compromising principles, companies that transcend are those that stand firm on their values. This means acting fairly and honestly in all interactions, whether with employees, customers or partners. An ethical culture not only builds trust and respect within the organization, but also enhances the company's reputation in society. Companies that act with integrity build lasting relationships based on trust, allowing them to make a positive impact far beyond their immediate operations.

The corporate culture for the common good is also marked by an attitude of service towards others. These companies are not only interested in their own success, but see themselves as part of a broader network of communities and social actors. Therefore, they actively engage with causes that matter. Whether through donations, volunteering or social responsibility initiatives, these companies look for ways to give something back to society. By getting involved in activities that benefit communities, they not only create a positive impact, but also strengthen the bond with their employees and customers, who feel more connected to a company that shares their values.

Of course, building a corporate culture for the common good is not something that can be achieved overnight. It requires constant commitment and a long-term vision. Company leaders must be the first to lead by example, acting in accordance with the principles they promote. In addition, it is important that the company's purpose and values are clearly communicated at all levels of the organization. Only when every person within the company understands and shares these principles will the culture be able to authentically flourish.

Transparency also plays a key role in this type of culture. Companies that are open and honest in their communication create an environment of trust and respect. This not only applies to the way they interact with their employees, but also with their customers and society at large. Transparency in business practices, decision-making and accountability reinforces the commitment to the common good and ensures that the company remains true to its values, even in difficult times.

In conclusion, a corporate culture for the common good is one that places people, ethics, sustainability, and social purpose at the center of all its activities. These companies understand that their success is intrinsically linked to the well-being of their employees, their customers, their communities, and the planet. They foster an inclusive and respectful work environment, invest in the growth of their employees, act ethically and responsibly, and actively engage in causes that improve society. By building a corporate culture that seeks the common good, companies not only succeed financially, but also create a positive and lasting impact on the world.

Collaboration and Strategic Alliances

Collaboration and strategic alliances are fundamental pillars for the success of any company that aspires to grow and leave a lasting mark. In an increasingly interconnected business world, no company can do everything on its own. Organizations that understand the importance of working together, joining forces, and creating strong alliances are the ones that manage to move forward more quickly, innovatively, and sustainably. Collaboration not only expands a company's capabilities, but also opens doors to new opportunities, markets, and knowledge that would otherwise be unattainable.

Collaboration isn't just a buzzword – it's a real and powerful strategy. When a company collaborates, it's not just about sharing resources, but also about sharing ideas, experiences and vision. A well-managed strategic alliance can be a source of innovation, helping both parties discover fresh approaches and solutions to complex problems. Furthermore, collaboration allows companies to complement each other, using their individual strengths to overcome any weaknesses. For example, a company that dominates in technology can ally itself with another that has a strong customer base, creating a winning combination that benefits both.

One of the biggest benefits of collaboration is the ability to access new markets. Strategic alliances can open the door to geographies and sectors where a company alone might not have the infrastructure or knowledge to enter. By partnering with a company that is local or experienced in that market, risks are reduced and the likelihood of success is increased. This is especially important in today's globalized world, where geographic barriers are increasingly easier to overcome, but where local knowledge remains key to success in new territories.

Collaboration can also be a source of savings and efficiency. By sharing resources, both human and financial, companies can reduce costs and streamline their operations. For example, a strategic alliance could allow two companies to share logistics or technology infrastructure, thereby reducing duplication of efforts and resources. This not only creates savings, but also improves operational efficiency, allowing both companies to focus their energies on what they do best. Instead of spending time and money developing something from scratch, they can leverage their partners' knowledge and capabilities to move faster.

However, not all strategic alliances are created equal, nor are all collaborations automatically successful. For a collaboration to work, there must be a clear alignment of goals and values. Companies must share a common vision and work towards a goal that benefits both parties. If interests are too misaligned or if one party is more interested in immediate gains without providing long-term value, the alliance risks failing. It is therefore crucial that companies take the time to carefully select their partners, ensuring that there is a cultural and strategic fit.

Trust is another essential ingredient in any successful collaboration. Without trust, any partnership is doomed to failure. Companies need to be open and transparent with each other, sharing the information necessary for both parties to make informed decisions. This transparency not only concerns the financial aspects, but also the way the company operates, the challenges it faces, and the expectations of each party. When companies trust each other, it is easier to resolve conflicts, adapt to changes, and find creative solutions to the problems that will inevitably arise.

Strategic alliances should not only benefit the companies involved, but also their customers. When two companies collaborate effectively, they can offer better products and services to their customers, as they combine the best of both worlds. Whether it is a more innovative product, a more efficient service, or a more personalized customer experience, collaboration can lead to results that neither company could have achieved on their own. In this sense, collaboration is not just a business strategy, but a way to generate greater value for customers, which is, at the end of the day, what drives the success of any company.

Furthermore, strategic partnerships can be key to long-term sustainability. In a world where resources are limited and global challenges such as climate change or social inequalities are becoming more evident, no company can solve these problems alone. Partnerships between companies, non-profit organizations, governments and other entities can be essential to address these challenges more effectively. Companies that commit to collaborating on sustainability issues are not only improving their own reputation, but are also contributing to the common good, creating a positive impact on society.

Collaboration doesn't always have to be between companies in the same industry. In fact, some of the most innovative and successful partnerships have emerged between companies from different industries that have found common ground in working together. For example, a technology company might collaborate with a healthcare company to develop new medical solutions, or a fashion company might partner with a technology company to integrate smart devices into its clothing. By joining forces with companies from other industries, solutions can be created that were never before imagined, taking innovation to a new level.

The process of forming strategic alliances can also be challenging. Companies must learn to negotiate and set clear terms from the beginning. A well-structured agreement should include details about each party's roles and responsibilities, how benefits and risks will be shared, and what will happen if the alliance doesn't work out as expected. These clear agreements not only help avoid misunderstandings, but they also provide a roadmap for collaboration. Companies must be prepared to invest time and resources into developing these relationships properly, as a successful strategic alliance doesn't happen overnight.

Finally, collaboration and strategic alliances are not static. For a partnership to remain successful, both parties must be willing to adapt and evolve over time. Market conditions change, business objectives adjust, and customer needs vary. A collaboration that was successful in the past may need adjustments to remain relevant. Companies that are flexible and willing to continually re-evaluate their partnerships are the ones that manage to maintain fruitful relationships over time.

In short, collaboration and strategic alliances are powerful tools for any company looking to grow, innovate and thrive in today's marketplace. By joining forces with others, companies can access new markets, improve their efficiency, generate innovation and deliver more value to their customers. However, for these alliances to be successful, it is critical that there is trust, transparency, a clear alignment of objectives and a willingness to adapt to change. Companies that understand this and invest in building strong, long-term relationships will be the ones that stay ahead of the curve, overcoming challenges and seizing the opportunities of the future.

Key Elements of Sustainable Success

Sustainable success is the kind of success that lasts over time, that does not depend on temporary factors or strokes of luck, but on a solid and well-thought-out construction that allows companies to remain competitive, profitable and responsible with the world around them. Achieving this kind of success is not just about doing things right in the present, but about making sure that what is done today will have a positive impact tomorrow. It is a long-term vision that considers the balance between economic growth, social well-being and care for the environment. To achieve this balance, it is essential to understand the key elements that allow a company to prosper sustainably.

The first key element is having a clear purpose. Companies that are successful in the long term do not focus solely on generating profits, but on a greater purpose that drives them to do something positive for society. This purpose can be related to improving people's quality of life, protecting the environment, or contributing to the development of communities. When a company has a clear purpose, its employees, customers, and partners can connect with that mission, which generates a much stronger sense of commitment and loyalty. In addition, a strong purpose also allows the company to stay on the right path, even when facing challenges or changes in the market.

Another key element is constant innovation. Companies that remain stagnant and do not adapt to market changes or new customer demands risk disappearing over time. Innovation does not always have to be radical or disruptive; sometimes small changes or improvements can make all the difference. The key is to always be on the lookout for opportunities to improve products, processes and services. This not only helps to stay competitive, but also allows companies to be more efficient and offer solutions that better fit customer needs. The ability to continuously innovate is one of the most important drivers of sustainable success.

Responsible resource management is also an essential pillar of long-term success. Companies that adopt sustainable practices, such as efficient use of natural resources, reducing waste and minimising their environmental impact, are not only protecting the planet, but also ensuring their own long-term survival. Unsustainable practices, such as excessive use of materials or pollution, can have disastrous consequences for both the natural environment and the company's reputation. In contrast, companies that are resource-conscious and adopt sustainable measures are often more efficient, reduce costs and gain the trust of consumers, who increasingly value brands that care about the environment.

A focus on people is another key component of sustainable success. A company is only as good as its team, which is why it is essential to create a work environment that promotes employee wellbeing and personal development. Successful companies are those that invest in their people, offering growth opportunities, training, and an environment where employees feel valued and motivated. A motivated team is not only more productive, but also more committed to the company's goals, which translates into better long-term results. In addition, talent retention is crucial for sustainability, as a high level of staff turnover can lead to inefficiencies and additional costs.

Customer relationships are also a key aspect of sustainable success. Companies that build strong, trusting relationships with their customers are the ones that manage to retain them over time. Instead of focusing solely on immediate sales, companies should be concerned with creating an exceptional customer experience that keeps consumers coming back again and again. Listening to customers' needs, offering solutions that truly add value to them, and staying connected with them in an authentic way are strategies that allow them to build long-term loyalty. When customers feel that a company truly cares about them and their needs, they are more likely to become brand advocates and recommend their products or services to others.

Another crucial element for sustainable success is the ability to adapt to change. We live in a world in constant transformation, where economic, social and technological conditions evolve rapidly. Companies that are able to adapt to these changes, anticipate trends and adjust their strategy as necessary are the ones that manage to stay relevant over time. This adaptability does not mean being reactive, but proactive, always being alert to what is happening in the environment and making informed decisions to stay ahead. The ability to be flexible and adjust to new realities is a competitive advantage that allows companies to survive and thrive in an uncertain environment.

Ethics and transparency are also critical to building lasting success. Companies that act ethically, are transparent in their practices, and are governed by sound principles build trust with their customers, employees, and partners. In a world where information circulates faster than ever, companies that are not transparent or that engage in unethical practices can suffer irreparable damage to their reputation. Conversely, those that behave with integrity and responsibility often attract more loyal customers and more engaged employees. Transparency in how decisions are made, how resources are managed, and how stakeholders are interacted with is key to building a solid foundation of trust.

Visionary leadership is another determining factor in sustainable success. Leaders of successful companies are those who not only have a clear vision of the future, but are also able to inspire their teams and guide them towards that future. A good leader does not focus solely on immediate results, but makes decisions with the long term in mind. Furthermore, a leader who cares about the well-being of his team, who is empathetic and who is committed to the company's values, is able to create an environment where people work with passion and commitment. Strong and conscious leadership is key to building a company that is not only profitable, but also sustainable and responsible.

The final key element of sustainable success is commitment to the community and environment in which the company operates. Companies do not exist in a vacuum, they are connected to the communities, people and ecosystems that surround them. Companies that care about the impact they generate, that look for ways to give something positive back to communities and that get involved in projects that benefit society, are the ones that manage to transcend and be seen as agents of positive change. This commitment not only improves the reputation of the company, but also creates a closer relationship with customers and other stakeholders, who value companies that care about more than just their own profits.

In conclusion, sustainable success is the result of a balanced approach that considers both economic and social and environmental aspects. Companies that have a clear purpose, that constantly innovate, that responsibly manage their resources, that value their people and that build strong relationships with their customers are the ones that manage to endure over time. In addition, the ability to adapt to change, act in an ethical and transparent manner, have visionary leadership and commit to the community are essential ingredients to build a success that is not only profitable, but also responsible and lasting. This type of success is the one that really matters, the one that leaves a positive mark on the world and on people, and that allows companies to prosper in harmony with their environment.

Innovation for Social Change

Innovation for social change is one of the most powerful forces that can transform the world. Throughout history, we have seen how innovative ideas have changed the way we live, work, and relate to each other. However, innovation should not only be focused on improving products or services to generate profits, but also on addressing the most pressing social problems and finding solutions that benefit the most vulnerable people and communities. This type of innovation has a deeper purpose, because it is about using ingenuity and creativity to solve the great social challenges we face, such as poverty, inequality, access to education and health care, or climate change.

Innovation for social change does not follow traditional market rules. It is not about creating something new just to attract consumers, but about creating something that has a real and positive impact on people's lives. This type of innovation can come in many forms, from creating new technologies to implementing business models that include those who are normally excluded from the economic system. The important thing is that innovation focuses on improving social well-being, making the benefits reach everyone, not just a few. A company that innovates with a social focus can create solutions that not only change its industry, but also transform entire communities.

A clear example of innovation for social change are technologies that seek to bring clean and affordable energy to regions where there was previously no access to electricity. In many developing countries, millions of people live without access to electricity, limiting their ability to improve their quality of life. However, thanks to innovations such as portable solar panels or decentralized power grids, it is now possible to provide renewable energy to remote communities efficiently and at low cost. This not only improves the living conditions of these people, but also helps reduce dependence on fossil fuels and combat climate change. These types of innovations show how technology can be a powerful tool for social progress.

Another area where innovation can have a significant impact is in education. In many parts of the world, millions of children do not have access to quality education, either due to a lack of resources, infrastructure or cultural barriers. However, through technological innovations such as online learning platforms or mobile applications that offer educational content, it is possible to reach these children and provide them with tools to learn, no matter where they are. These solutions can be especially useful in rural areas or in communities that have been historically marginalized. By offering more accessible and quality education, innovation can break the cycle of poverty and open new opportunities for future generations.

In the health field, innovation for social change can also make a big difference. Lack of access to healthcare is a global problem affecting millions of people, especially in rural areas or developing countries. However, with the emergence of technologies such as telemedicine, wearable health monitoring devices and remote diagnostics, new ways of delivering healthcare to those who previously lacked it are being created. These innovations not only improve people's quality of life, but also reduce the burden on healthcare systems, allowing for more efficient and equitable care. Innovation in healthcare has the potential to save lives and make medical services more accessible to all.

Social innovation is not just about technology; it can also be a matter of changing mindsets and business models. For example, companies that adopt fair trade practices are innovating by creating a system that pays living wages to producers in developing countries. This approach not only improves the living conditions of workers, but also creates a more ethical and sustainable business model. By paying fair prices and offering better working conditions, these companies are promoting significant social change, while also offering high-quality products to consumers. This type of innovation shows that it is possible to create successful businesses that are also socially responsible.

Social entrepreneurship is another form of innovation that is driving change. More and more entrepreneurs are starting businesses with the goal of addressing specific social problems. These entrepreneurs are not only looking to generate economic profits, but also to maximize the positive social impact of their companies. Whether they are creating eco-friendly products, developing accessible healthcare solutions, or helping marginalized communities integrate into the economy, social entrepreneurs are proving that it is possible to innovate profitably and responsibly. This new generation of business leaders is redefining what it means to be successful in business, placing social good at the center of their activities.

For innovation for social change to be effective, it is also important that companies and entrepreneurs work in collaboration with governments, non-governmental organizations and the communities they seek to help. The most effective solutions are those that are developed with a deep understanding of local problems and that have the active participation of those who will benefit from that innovation. Collaboration between different sectors is key to ensure that solutions are not only technically viable, but also culturally appropriate and sustainable in the long term. Social innovation must be a joint effort, with all actors working towards the same goal.

Social change can also be driven from within companies, through innovative corporate policies that promote equality, diversity and inclusion. Companies that innovate in their employment practices, offering equal opportunities for all employees, regardless of gender, race or origin, are contributing to important social change. Furthermore, by fostering an inclusive work environment, companies not only improve the morale and productivity of their employees, but also attract a more diverse and skilled talent base. This type of innovation not only has a positive impact within the company, but also sends a powerful message to society about the importance of equality and justice.

As businesses and entrepreneurs continue to innovate for social change, it's also critical to measure the impact of these innovations. It's not just about having good intentions, but about making sure that the solutions are actually improving people's lives. There are many tools and methods for measuring social impact, from surveys and case studies to financial and wellbeing metrics. By measuring impact effectively, businesses can learn what's working and what needs improvement, ensuring that their innovations have the greatest possible effect on society.

Ultimately, innovation for social change is a powerful tool that can transform the world we live in. Whether through technology, new business models, or the implementation of fairer and more equitable policies, the possibilities are endless. What is most important is that innovation is guided by a greater purpose, one that puts people and the planet at the center of the strategy. Companies that manage to combine innovation with social commitment are the ones that truly make a difference, not only for their shareholders, but for humanity as a whole. Innovating for social change is, ultimately, a way to create a better future for all.

Measuring Social Impact

Measuring the social impact of a company or project is essential to know if it is really achieving the change it seeks in society. It is not just about doing good deeds or having good intentions, but about being able to clearly evaluate whether the initiatives are generating tangible and positive results for people, communities and the environment. For many companies, measuring social impact may seem complicated, but it is a crucial part of ensuring that the social purpose does not remain an idea, but is translated into real improvements.

The first step in measuring social impact is to clearly define objectives. This means that a company or project must be very clear about what it wants to achieve. For example, if a company wants to reduce poverty in a rural community through job creation, it must set concrete goals, such as how many jobs it intends to create, in what time frame, and how these jobs will help improve people's quality of life. Having these clear objectives makes it possible to measure whether the expected results are being achieved and to make adjustments if necessary. Without well-defined goals, it is difficult to know whether efforts are having the desired impact.

Once the objectives are clear, the next step is to identify the metrics that will be used to measure the impact. Metrics are specific indicators that show how progress is being made towards the objectives. For example, if a company is working to improve education in a community, some relevant metrics could be school attendance rate, student academic performance, or the number of new teachers hired. These metrics provide a clear and quantifiable view of the impact. It is important that the metrics are relevant, easy to measure, and aligned with the project objectives.

However, not all metrics have to be numerical. Social impact can also be measured qualitatively, i.e. by looking at how people's lives have changed or how the well-being of a community has improved. Surveys, interviews or case studies can be useful tools to obtain this type of information. For example, in a health project, a qualitative metric could be how people perceive the improvement in their quality of life after receiving medical care. Personal stories can be just as valuable as numbers when it comes to measuring social impact, because they show the change from a human perspective.

Measuring social impact is not something that should be done only at the end of a project. It is an ongoing process that should be carried out over time to assess progress and make necessary adjustments. That is why it is important to carry out periodic measurements to see if efforts are on the right track or if the strategy needs to be changed. Sometimes, results are not seen immediately, so it is essential to be patient and persistent. But measuring continuously allows for learning and improvement, ensuring that resources are used in the best possible way to maximize impact.

Another important aspect of measuring social impact is transparency. Companies and organizations need to be open and honest about the results they are achieving. It won't always be easy to show that great progress is being made, especially on complex projects that address deep social problems. However, being transparent about successes and challenges builds trust with affected people and communities, as well as with investors and partners. In addition, transparency allows others to learn from experiences and mistakes, which contributes to the improvement of future social initiatives.

Measuring social impact can also help attract more support, both financial and community-based. When a company can clearly show the positive impact it is having, it is more likely to get additional investments or donations, because potential funders see that their money is being used effectively. What's more, measuring impact can also inspire more people to join the cause, whether as employees, volunteers, or advocates for the company's mission. When people see clear evidence that an organization is making a difference, they are more inclined to support it.

Technology has made measuring social impact much easier and more accurate. Today, there are digital tools that allow you to collect data in real time, analyze trends, and generate detailed reports on project progress. These tools not only make measurement easier, but also help identify areas for improvement more quickly. In addition, technology allows data to be collected in a more efficient manner, which reduces costs and time spent on evaluation. Using technology to measure social impact is not only useful for businesses, but also for non-profit organizations and government projects that seek to have a significant social impact.

It is important to remember that measuring social impact benefits not only companies or projects, but also the communities and people who receive the help. When a company measures impact appropriately, it can ensure that it is responding to people's real needs and adjusting its actions to have a greater positive effect. This also helps to avoid "welfare" - that is, offering superficial solutions that do not solve the underlying problems. Measuring social impact allows for a deeper and more effective approach, focused on generating lasting change.

In short, measuring social impact is a key process for any company or project that has a purpose beyond economic profit. It is the tool that allows you to evaluate whether your efforts are achieving the change you are seeking in society and how you can improve to maximize that impact. From defining clear objectives and establishing metrics, to using technological tools and being transparent with the results, each step in measuring social impact is important to ensure that actions translate into real benefit for people and the planet. And at the end of the day, that is the real reason why purpose-driven companies work: to make a positive and meaningful change in the world.

Evelyn Wright

Beyond Sustainability

When we talk about sustainability, we typically think about how businesses and individuals can make an effort to reduce their negative impact on the environment. This includes things like using fewer resources, reducing carbon emissions, recycling more, and trying not to harm the planet. Sustainability has been a central topic in conversations about social and environmental responsibility for years. However, in today's world, where global challenges are becoming more complex and urgent, sustainability is no longer enough. Now, more than ever, there is a need to go beyond sustainability and focus on a vision that not only minimizes harm, but also seeks to regenerate and improve our environment.

Moving beyond sustainability means moving away from thinking only in terms of "doing less harm" and starting to think about how we can "do more good." It's not enough to avoid destroying natural resources; we now need to find ways to restore ecosystems, regenerate soils, purify air and water, and give back to nature more than we take from it. This approach is known as regenerative economics, and it goes a step beyond sustainable practices.

Regenerative economics doesn't just preserve what we already have, but focuses on repairing what has been damaged and creating systems that are prosperous for all living things, including future generations.

A clear example of how to go beyond sustainability is regenerative design in agriculture. While sustainable agriculture seeks to minimize the environmental impact of farming practices, regenerative agriculture aims to improve soil health, increase biodiversity, and capture carbon rather than releasing it. Farmers who adopt these practices not only avoid using harmful chemicals, but also work to regenerate the land, which in turn improves food production, reduces the impact of climate change, and creates a healthier cycle between ecosystems and people. This approach has a long-term positive impact on both the environment and farming communities.

Companies that take a regenerative approach are also finding that this model is a source of innovation and competitive advantage. Rather than simply complying with environmental regulations, these companies are designing products, services, and processes that have a positive impact on the planet. For example, some companies are developing biodegradable products that not only do not harm the environment, but also help regenerate it. There are also companies that are using waste as raw material to create new products, closing the production loop and reducing the amount of waste that ends up in landfills. These initiatives are not only good for the planet, but they also open up new business opportunities.

Another important aspect of going beyond sustainability is rethinking traditional business models. Businesses of the future must not only be sustainable, but also regenerative and restorative in their approach. This means that they must create shared value, not only for their shareholders, but for all stakeholders, including local communities, employees, suppliers and the environment. A regenerative business model is based on the idea that business success should not depend on exploiting natural resources or people, but on creating a system in which everyone can thrive together. This approach also fosters greater resilience, as businesses that take care of their natural and social resources are better able to adapt to changes in the market and environment.

The concept of regeneration can also be applied to cities and communities. Rather than simply reducing energy or water consumption, cities that take a regenerative approach are looking for ways to improve the well-being of their inhabitants through solutions that restore urban ecosystems. This includes creating green spaces that improve air quality, encourage biodiversity, and provide recreational areas for people. It also includes implementing transportation systems that are not only efficient, but also help reduce pollution and promote a healthier lifestyle. These initiatives not only make cities more sustainable, but also make them more livable and resilient places.

Going beyond sustainability also involves a change in mindset. It is not just about reducing the harm we cause, but about taking active responsibility for improving the world we live in. It is necessary for businesses, governments and individuals to adopt a regeneration mindset, where every decision we make is geared towards improving the quality of life of current and future generations. This requires us to stop seeing nature as a resource that we can exploit and start seeing it as a partner with whom we must collaborate to ensure a prosperous future. This regeneration mindset also encourages innovation, as it forces us to rethink our ways of production and consumption in a more creative and sustainable way.

The regenerative approach benefits not only the environment, but also people. Companies that invest in regenerative practices are creating more meaningful and rewarding jobs for their employees, as they feel like they are contributing to something bigger than simply generating profits. Additionally, by involving communities in their regenerative efforts, these companies are strengthening relationships with their customers, who increasingly value brands that are committed to social and environmental well-being. In this way, going beyond sustainability is not only good for the planet, but also for business.

In short, sustainability is no longer enough in a world facing such huge environmental and social challenges. Businesses and individuals must go further, adopting a regenerative approach that not only minimises harm, but also restores and enhances the natural and social systems on which we all depend. This approach requires an innovative and collaborative mindset, one that sees nature as a partner and not as a resource to be exploited. Going beyond sustainability is a commitment to the future, to the idea that we can create a world in which people, businesses and the environment thrive together. True innovation is not about doing less harm, but about finding ways to do more good, so that the positive impact of our actions extends into the long term and for generations to come.

The Value of a Company in a Purpose-Driven Economy

The value of a company in a purpose-driven economy goes far beyond its revenue and profits. In the past, the measure of a company's success was purely financial: the more money it made, the more successful it was considered. Today, however, expectations about what constitutes a valuable company have changed. We live in a world where people, consumers, and investors are looking for more than just products or services. They want to know that companies are making a positive contribution to society and that they have a purpose greater than simply making a profit.

The concept of a "purpose economy" refers to an economic model where companies not only seek to maximize profits, but also create a positive social, environmental and human impact. Rather than focusing exclusively on short-term profits, companies in a purpose economy are guided by a set of values that benefit all stakeholders: employees, customers, communities and the planet. This does not mean that financial value ceases to be important, but that business success is measured in a more holistic way, considering both economic and social impact.

A company in a purpose economy understands that having a clear and genuine purpose increases its long-term value. Consumers, especially younger generations, prefer to support brands that align with their values. They want to know that the companies they interact with are doing the right thing, whether through responsible production, respecting human rights, supporting social causes, or protecting the environment. Purpose is not a slogan or a marketing campaign; it is at the core of a company's identity, giving meaning to its existence and defining its actions.

A clear example of how a company can have a meaningful purpose is when its operations and products are designed to solve social or environmental problems. Imagine a company that makes clothes, but instead of doing it in a conventional way, it uses recycled materials, guarantees fair working conditions for its workers and donates part of its profits to reforestation programs. This company does not just sell clothes; it sells an idea, a commitment to the well-being of the planet and people. The value of this company, therefore, is not only measured by the number of garments it sells, but by the positive impact it has on the environment and the communities where it operates.

Another important aspect of companies in a purpose economy is their ability to attract and retain talent. Today's employees aren't just looking for good salaries; they also want to work for companies that allow them to feel like they're contributing to something bigger. They want to feel like their work has meaning and that they're making a difference. When a company has a clear purpose, it can inspire its employees, improve their motivation, and increase their loyalty. A team that is committed to the company's purpose not only works harder, but is also more creative and innovative, which generates even greater value for the organization.

Leadership also plays a critical role in the value of a purpose-driven company. Leaders who embrace and promote a values-based approach are able to guide their teams toward a shared vision that focuses not only on financial results, but also on the positive impact they can make on the world. An inspiring leader understands that profitability and purpose are not opposing goals, but can coexist and reinforce each other. As purpose drives innovation and engagement, the company grows sustainably and builds a strong reputation based on trust and integrity.

In a purpose economy, transparency is key. Companies can no longer hide behind empty promises or policies they don't deliver on. Consumers and other stakeholders expect companies to be honest about their practices, how they treat their employees, how they produce their goods, and what they do to minimize their environmental impact. Being transparent not only builds trust, but it also strengthens the relationship between the company and its community. Companies that are open about their challenges and progress on purpose issues generate a higher level of engagement both internally and externally.

A company's value is also reflected in its partnerships and collaborations. Rather than fiercely competing with other companies, purpose-driven organizations often seek out strategic partnerships that allow them to multiply their impact. These partnerships can be with other companies, nonprofits, governments, or local communities. Working together toward a common goal increases positive impact and demonstrates that the company is committed to real change, not just its own agenda. This collaborative approach also allows companies to constantly learn and improve, elevating their value and ability to adapt in an ever-changing economic and social environment.

A company with a well-defined purpose is also more resilient to crises. Companies that focus only on short-term profits can be vulnerable to market changes, global economic problems, or social crises. However, purpose-driven companies have a solid foundation of values that allows them to better adapt and respond more effectively to these challenges. In addition, purpose-driven companies typically have a higher level of trust from their customers, employees, and investors, which gives them greater room to maneuver during difficult times.

It's no coincidence that purpose-driven companies often fare better in the long run. As more consumers and business partners choose to work with companies that align with their values, purpose-driven companies can grow and thrive in an economy that increasingly demands social and environmental responsibility. This growth is reflected not only in the financial numbers, but also in the creation of shared value – value that benefits all stakeholders and promotes positive change in the world.

In conclusion, the value of a company in a purpose economy is not measured solely by its profitability. It is a value that is built from the combination of its actions, its impact on society and the environment, and its ability to improve people's lives. Companies that understand this and that embrace genuine purpose in their operations are positioned to succeed, not only financially, but also in terms of their relevance and legacy in an increasingly conscious and demanding world. In the purpose economy, true value is in doing the right thing, not only for the present, but also for the future.

Preparing the Next Generation of Conscious Entrepreneurs

Preparing the next generation of conscious entrepreneurs is a crucial task in a rapidly changing world facing increasingly complex challenges. Global issues such as climate change, social inequality and the natural resource crisis require new forms of business leadership. We cannot rely solely on traditional business models that have been focused almost exclusively on economic growth and profit maximization. Future generations of entrepreneurs will need a much broader mindset and an approach that combines financial success with social and environmental responsibility.

One of the first steps in preparing the next generation of conscious entrepreneurs is to educate them in values that promote collective well-being. Business schools, universities and business training programs must teach not only technical skills such as accounting or marketing, but also instill ethical and sustainability principles. Future leaders must learn to make decisions that consider not only the short-term impact on financial balance sheets, but also the long-term consequences on people and the planet. This requires comprehensive training that combines theory with practical experiences that allow them to see the real impact of their decisions.

In addition to formal education, it is vital that young entrepreneurs have the opportunity to get involved in social impact projects from an early age. By participating in initiatives that seek to solve problems in their communities or improve the environment, young people develop a deeper awareness of the world they live in and the needs that need to be addressed. This not only helps them better understand the challenges, but also allows them to develop empathy, an essential trait in a conscious entrepreneur. When an entrepreneur understands and feels the struggles of others, they are better equipped to design business solutions that not only generate economic value, but also improve people's lives.

Another crucial aspect of preparing the next generation of conscious entrepreneurs is fostering a sustainable innovation mindset. Instead of blindly following traditional formulas for creating products and services, young entrepreneurs should be encouraged to think disruptively, finding ways to do things better and more efficiently, without harming the environment. Sustainable innovation focuses on developing products that not only meet the needs of the present, but also preserve resources for future generations. This involves making use of clean technologies, adopting circular economy models, and designing solutions that reduce waste and promote efficient use of resources.

Ethical leadership must also be a fundamental part of the training of these new entrepreneurs. Integrity and transparency are more important than ever in a world where people are demanding more accountability from businesses. Conscious entrepreneurs must not only guide their own companies with these values, but also be able to inspire others to do the same. This means leading by example, promoting business practices that are fair, equitable, and respectful to everyone involved in the process, from employees to suppliers to customers. How a leader treats people and handles ethical challenges defines not only their personal reputation, but also the legacy of their company.

Networks of mentors and role models play a critical role in developing conscious entrepreneurs. Young entrepreneurs often benefit greatly from having guides who have already walked the path of responsible entrepreneurship. Having access to mentors who have successfully applied social responsibility principles in their companies gives new leaders valuable perspective and helps them avoid common mistakes. In addition, mentors can inspire the next generation to be brave and stand firm in their convictions, even when ethical and responsible decisions may not seem to be the easiest or most lucrative in the short term.

Collaboration is also an essential skill for future-conscious entrepreneurs. Rather than seeing other companies as direct competition, the next generation must learn to work collaboratively with other players, including competitors, governments, and nonprofits, to solve global problems. The challenges facing the world today are too big for any one company to solve alone. Collaborating with others to achieve shared goals not only increases the chances of success, but also creates a bigger and more meaningful impact on the world. This mindset of collaboration over competition is key to building a more just and sustainable future.

Future-conscious businesses must also understand the importance of equity and inclusion in all aspects of their business. Preparing the next generation of entrepreneurs includes teaching them that businesses must be diverse and reflect the society in which they operate. Diversity of thought, experience, and background not only enriches decision-making, but is also crucial to creating products and services that meet the needs of a diverse audience. A conscious entrepreneur values and encourages inclusion within their team, ensuring that everyone has the opportunity to contribute and be heard.

Another powerful tool for the next generation of conscious entrepreneurs is the power of technology. New technologies have the potential to solve many of humanity's most pressing problems, from access to clean energy to improving education and health in marginalized communities. However, future business leaders must learn to use technology responsibly and ethically. This means not only seeking efficiency and progress, but also ensuring that technology is developed and used in ways that respect human rights, protect privacy, and do not widen inequality. In this sense, conscious entrepreneurs must be advocates for a balanced and fair use of technologies.

Finally, it is critical that the next generation of entrepreneurs take a long-term view. The decisions they make today can have repercussions for decades. They must therefore be willing to think ahead, foresee the potential consequences of their actions and commit to sustainable development. It is not just about generating quick results or chasing immediate success; it is about building companies that endure and continue to generate a positive impact long after the founder has retired. This kind of legacy mindset is essential to ensure that the companies of tomorrow are not only profitable, but also responsible and relevant.

In short, preparing the next generation of conscious entrepreneurs requires a holistic approach that encompasses values education, sustainable innovation, ethical leadership, collaboration and a long-term vision. By equipping young entrepreneurs with these tools, we will not only be preparing the leaders of the future, but we will also be ensuring that the companies of tomorrow are more humane, responsible and committed to the well-being of society and the planet. This generation has the potential to change the world, and it is up to us to give them the skills and knowledge to do so consciously and effectively.

Legacy

The concept of legacy is fundamental when talking about a company or an entrepreneur that seeks to transcend beyond financial success. A legacy is not just about what a person leaves in the world when they leave, but about how their actions, decisions, and values continue to impact future generations. For a conscious entrepreneur, legacy goes far beyond the accumulation of wealth or personal recognition. It is the lasting mark left on society, on people's lives, and on the environment. Legacy is built over time, and is reflected in the way a company operates, the values it promotes, and the solutions it provides to the world's problems.

When an entrepreneur cares about the legacy he will leave behind, his vision shifts from short-term to long-term. It is no longer just about maximizing profits or dominating the market for a few years, but about building something that will last, that will remain relevant and valuable even when he is no longer involved in the day-to-day running of the business. This kind of long-term vision is essential to creating a positive and lasting impact, because it forces leaders to think about the consequences of their decisions, not only in financial terms, but also in terms of their social and environmental impact. In this way, legacy is not an accidental outcome, but an intentional goal that is worked on every day.

An important part of legacy is the culture a company creates. Company culture is made up of the values, beliefs, and behaviors that guide the organization. If a company promotes honesty, fairness, and respect, those qualities become part of its identity and are passed on to future generations of employees, customers, and partners. On the other hand, if a company focuses solely on profit, without considering the well-being of its employees or the impact of its operations on society, its legacy will be very different. Conscious business owners must be very careful about the culture they cultivate, as it will be an essential part of what they leave behind.

A meaningful legacy is also built through the positive impact a company has on its environment. It is not just about meeting minimum expectations, but about making a real, measurable difference. This can include environmental initiatives, such as reducing the carbon footprint or promoting the use of renewable energy, or social programs that improve the lives of the communities in which the company operates. Companies that leave a lasting legacy do not just limit themselves to operating responsibly, but actively seek to create shared value – an approach where both the company and society benefit equally. This type of approach is key to building a legacy that endures and is appreciated over time.

Legacy is also intrinsically linked to innovation. Companies that make a mark not only adapt to market trends, but are pioneers in creating solutions that change the world for the better. Innovation is not just about creating new products or services, but about finding ways to do things more efficiently, more responsibly and more consciously. An entrepreneur who leaves a lasting legacy is one who, instead of following the easy path or the most profitable one in the short term, bets on change, evolution and progress. This type of innovation not only has an immediate impact, but lays the foundation for future generations to continue improving and transforming the industry and society.

Another critical part of a legacy is how people are treated inside and outside the company. An entrepreneur who leaves a positive legacy is one who cares about their employees, treating them with dignity and respect, and providing them with opportunities to grow both personally and professionally. They also care about their customers, offering products and services that truly improve their lives, and about the community, contributing to the general well-being. When a company operates with these principles, it leaves a lasting impression on all those it interacts with. Employees will talk about that company as a place where they truly mattered, customers will remember how its products made a difference in their lives, and communities will feel that the company was a force for good.

Leadership also plays a central role in creating a legacy. Business leaders are not only responsible for the day-to-day decisions that affect the direction of the company, but they are also the guardians of its vision and mission. A leader who cares about his legacy ensures that his company is aligned with the right values and that his actions reflect his principles. This type of leadership is inspiring and mobilizes others to carry on with the same dedication and commitment. A good leader is aware that his influence goes beyond his term of office and strives to develop other leaders who can continue his work with the same passion and responsibility.

Legacy is not always measured in numbers or immediate achievements, but in the impact it has over time. Often, the smallest and seemingly insignificant actions can have the most profound impact. For example, a business decision that at the time seemed inconsequential, such as a commitment to reducing plastic waste or ensuring fair working conditions, can become an example for other companies and industries to follow. In this way, an entrepreneur's legacy not only influences their own company, but can inspire change across an entire industry and society at large. That's the power of a well-crafted legacy: its ability to multiply and expand beyond its original boundaries.

A successful legacy also requires planning. It's not about waiting for things to simply fall into place, but about being proactive in creating an impact that transcends. Entrepreneurs who want to leave a legacy must think strategically about how they want to be remembered and what kind of company they want to endure after them. This means setting clear goals, making conscious decisions, and ensuring that purpose and values are always at the heart of operations. A legacy is not something that is created overnight, but rather is carefully built over time, with every decision, every action, and every step taken.

Finally, a company's legacy is deeply connected to its ability to evolve and adapt. The world is constantly changing, and companies that leave a lasting legacy are those that are not afraid to adjust to new realities and challenges. A strong legacy doesn't mean clinging to old ways of doing things, but rather being willing to continually learn, grow, and improve. By doing so, a company can remain relevant and valuable for a long time, reinforcing its positive impact and ability to inspire others.

In short, the legacy of an entrepreneur or a company is the mark it leaves on the world. It is not just about the profits made, but about how it contributed to the well-being of society, how it treated people, and how it preserved the planet for future generations. A lasting legacy is built with responsibility, a long-term vision, and a genuine commitment to improving the world. It is a testament to the values and principles of those who build it, and its true value is measured by the positive impact it continues to have even when its creators are no longer present.